Scrolls Are Easy

By
LAVERNE E. BRESCIA

SECOND EDITION

An important note:

This second edition of "Scrolls Are Easy" has been published by the original author's daughter and granddaughter.

First published in 1964 by Passantino Printing Co., Inc.
250 W. 49th St., N.Y., N.Y. 10019
Second printing 2014 by Judith Brescia-Keenan and Nancy Bunt
© 1964 Laverne E. Brescia
© 2014 Judith Anne Keenan & Nancy Bunt
Book design by Nancy Bunt

ISBN-13: 978-0615955599
ISBN-10: 0615955592

Printed in USA
by Judith Brescia-Keenan & Nancy Bunt

Original 1964 Booklet Dedication

This booklet is dedicated to my husband for his patience and encouragement throughout my endeavor.

Contents

Introduction

"Enthusiasm is one of the most powerful engines of success. When you do a thing, do it with all your might. Put your whole soul into it. Stamp it with your own personality. Nothing great was ever achieved without enthusiasm"

— *Ralph Waldo Emerson*

This is exactly what Laverne Brescia did with her passion for rug hooking. She shared her enthusiasm for this beautiful craft with many people through the exhibits where her work was displayed, and through her teaching others about it. Laverne's heart and soul was in each piece she created. The commitment she had to the formation of an intricate design was immeasurable, and it showed in the final product. Rug hooking is a true art, where the artist makes the design come alive.

As Laverne advanced in her craft, she discovered valuable techniques and skills that could enhance the quality of her work and the work of others. This is why she first wrote "Scrolls Are Easy" in 1964. She wanted to share her passion and her knowledge with the rug hooking community.

We are honored today to be part of keeping her passion alive with this second edition of "Scrolls Are Easy".

- Judy & Nancy

In Laverne's Words:

After hooking rugs for nearly fifteen years, scrolls were still very difficult for me. I knew how they should look but the finished result was never quite pleasing. Looking around at others work, I discovered that many teachers and students felt the same way. Beautiful rug patterns were not being made simply because the women were afraid to attempt difficult scrolls. I decided that the only way to lick the problem was to look it straight in the eye.

For sometime I'd been toying with an idea for a new type of dyeing for scrolls; but I didn't do too much with it until I was asked to take part in a dye session at the McGown Teachers Workshop at South Lancaster, Mass. The colors obtained were pleasing but it wasn't until asked to repeat the dye session at the McGown Teachers Southern Workshop that I decided that it was one thing to dye colors but another to use them. With a sample scroll on burlap, I started hooking. Imagine my surprise and pleasure to find that using the method of dyeing which will be described in this book, made scrolls very easy and fun to do. The dyeing is really overdyeing as colors are placed one on top of the other. This has the effect of making shades seem softer. Remember these colors will come out differently than mixing dyes together in a pan. Each dye is placed separately on your strip, one dye over the other. Pastels as well as white and beige are used.

The Equipment Needed

Before you start dyeing, make yourself a coat hanger as follows: Get a heavy wire coat hanger and sew a piece of muslin across the straight arm (see Fig. 1 below). This will give you something to which you can anchor your materials.

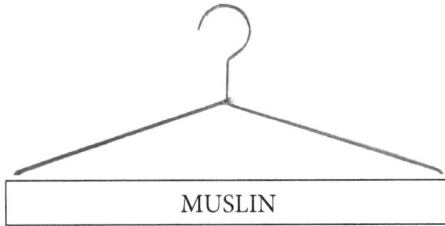

MUSLIN

Fig. 1

1. Four strips each 3x16 or 3x18 (size depends on length of scroll) of white, beige, yellow, pink, blue and green materials.
2. Seven large safety pins, 1½".
3. Six small safety pins.
4. Six ½" squares or snips of each color for markers.
5. Three small cups for dyes (custard cups are just right).
6. One and one-half cups of white vinegar.
7. One large oval dishpan - large enough to accommodate coat hanger.
8. One pair of tongs.
9. Three dyes.
10. Rubber gloves.
11. Detergent.

You will notice that each formula consists of three dyes. Put each measured amount of dry dye in a custard cup.

How To Prepare Materials

The length of the material is determined by the length of the finger or projection multiplied by four. If you hook high allow an extra inch to strip. Wet your pastels in a detergent solution and then pin to muslin on coat hanger with large safety pins (see Fig. 2 below).

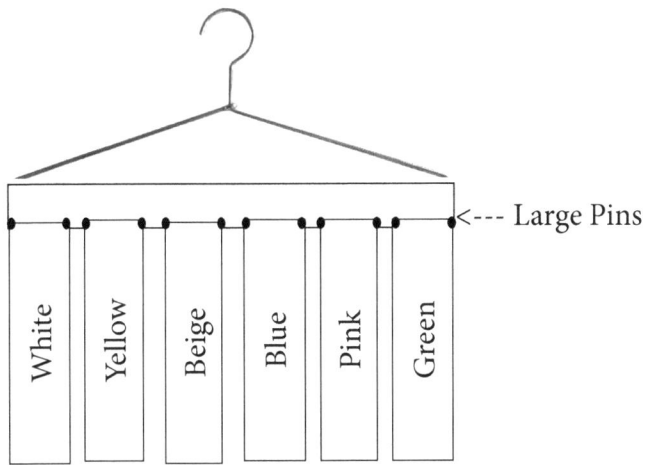

Fig. 2

It is a good idea to develop a system in which the pastels are always arranged in the same order, such as white, yellow, beige, blue, pink and green (see Fig. 2). In this manner, if you should forget to place a marker on a swatch it will be easier to identify the color you have dyed over. If your pastels are too dark they will not turn out as nice as paler shades. Bleed them out with a weak detergent solution before you start to dye. Since we cannot get as much white or beige as we used to, this is an excellent way of utilizing other shades.

Technique Of Dyeing

The formula used is as follows:
No. 1. Gold, ¼ teaspoon of dry dye
No. 2. Woodrose, ¼ teaspoon of dry dye
No. 3. Bronze green, ¼ teaspoon minus ⅟₃₂ of dry dye.

Place your No. 1 dye (gold) in your dishpan which is three quarters full of boiling water. Stir and add ½ cup of white vinegar. Keep heat high while dyeing as it penetrates faster. This dye is brought to the top of the material. That is, the entire strip is to be dyed in the gold. You have 24 pieces of material on the hanger so the dye will be taken up pretty fast. However, your lower ends (the first to touch the dye solution) should be darker in color. With your hands (in gloves) separate top of strips so that the dye will penetrate evenly. Hold the hanger or place it at the side of the pan (not in the pan), let boil for five minutes until the water is clear. Lift the hanger and materials out of the water and add No. 2 dye which in this formula is woodrose. Stir and add another ½ cup of white vinegar. Dip dye again but this time your dye is to come THREE FOURTHS (¾) of the way up the strip. Keep your materials moving up and down gently so that you will not get a line. When the water is clear lift up the coat hanger and add No. 3 dye, bronze green. Stir and add last ½ cup of white vinegar. This dye comes only ONE HALF (½) way up the strip and it takes longer to get the dye into the material. Be patient and when your solution is about the color of weak tea quickly overdye the ENTIRE strip. This overdyeing tones down the top colors. The dye solution should be almost clear, and if you wish you can drop the entire swatch in the pan and boil a few minutes. I have found that it takes about one half hour to dye this swatch and I don't usually boil it any longer. In fact, I have tried to boil out color from one of these swatches and found the color was fast. You have added enough vinegar to set the colors permanently.

Remove the coat hanger with the materials still pinned on and rinse in tepid water. Unpin the white and with the small safety pin put through the marker, pin to the four pieces of white. This puts the marker to the back of the swatch and it will stay until the swatch has been used up. Repeat this with each of your colors and hang them to dry this way. The colors are all closely related and they would be difficult to identify IF NOT MARKED.

In some localities where there is hard water my formulas may be too bright.

If this is so, use ⅟₃₂ teaspoon less of each dye. After dyeing many different color combinations, I have found that if you CLEAR the water of dye with each color you do not have to watch the color wheel. I might add that you cannot start with a strong dye at the top and expect weaker dyes to show at the middle and bottom. Start with a weak dye at the top and go toward stronger colors. At the end of this book (pages 39-42) you will find some of the color combinations that I have tried out.

1906 Cadillac
Laverne Brescia Photo 1968

How To Plan The Scroll

Your materials are now dyed. Study the scroll. I have a definition of scrolls which gives my students a better understanding of them. Scrolls can be considered as either a FINGER SCROLL or a FIST SCROLL. A finger scroll is one where the fingers or projections fan out from the center. A fist scroll is one where the fingers fold over on the center or palm such as the scroll on the U.S. dollar bill. If the scroll is a finger scroll it probably has some knobs and perhaps a vein which will be discussed later. Look at your swatches again. Usually, when you dye over six pastels one color will seem a bit foreign to the others. Instead of mixing this color next to the others why not make it a leading lady, using it for a turnover or a knob. *In both, "Forever Young" (Pages 25-26) and "Gainsborough" (Pages 27-29) it was the blue. If there is a vein in the scroll, make it very inconspicuous using a piece of dip dyed material. Lighten the vein at the top and darken toward the base. Your scroll will be colorful enough without playing up the vein.

Lay out your various swatches and decide where each color looks best. If white is used for one finger, tone down the next with beige, etc. I am referring to the color you dyed over and that is one reason your markers are so important. By placing the various colors roughly on the scroll fingers you can get an idea of how the colors will appear when hooked. Juggle them around until you have a pleasing pattern. It isn't necessary to use the same color on each side of the scroll but they should be balanced. After one scroll has been completed, the duplicate should be exactly the same.

* Note: Some of the old photos in this publication make it difficult to see the colors. Visit www.ScrollsAreEasy.com for examples of rugs in full color.

How To Hook Your Swatches

To make a large knob, break off the lightest part of seven cut strips. Start at "A" and hook as far as the strip will go (see Fig. 3). Take second piece and start one stitch above "A" and hook as far as it will go. It probably will be one stitch beyond the previous strip. Continue doing this with all seven pieces, always starting one stitch beyond the previous row. When you have finished you will have a crescent of your lightest color on knob edge. Take a fresh cut strip and starting at "B" (see Fig. 3) with light end, hook around knob edge to base of throat which automatically gets darker. The darker ends left from the crescent strips can be used under the knob from "A" to "C" (see Fig. 3).

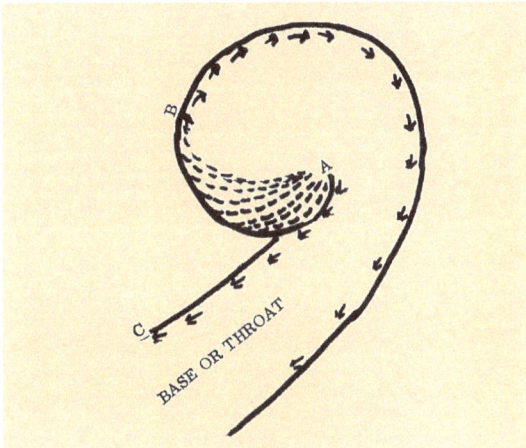

Fig. 3

Original 1964 Book Image

To make the fingers of the scroll start with the lightest end of the strip at the tip and hook in contour to base (see Fig. 4, page 20). Each finger will be made with a different pastel but the base of each will be about the same color and all will blend together along center of scroll. It is simple to do as your transition of color is all on one strip. Just remember to follow the vein if present or the outline of finger. Again I say you MUST HOOK IN CONTOUR. In some scrolls you may find some of the fingers are broad and flat. This type is often found in the fist type scroll. It is made by starting at the center of the top with the lightest shade and working along both edges of finger, first the right side and then the left (see Fig. 5, page 20). Break off light ends and match shades as you progress toward center to base.

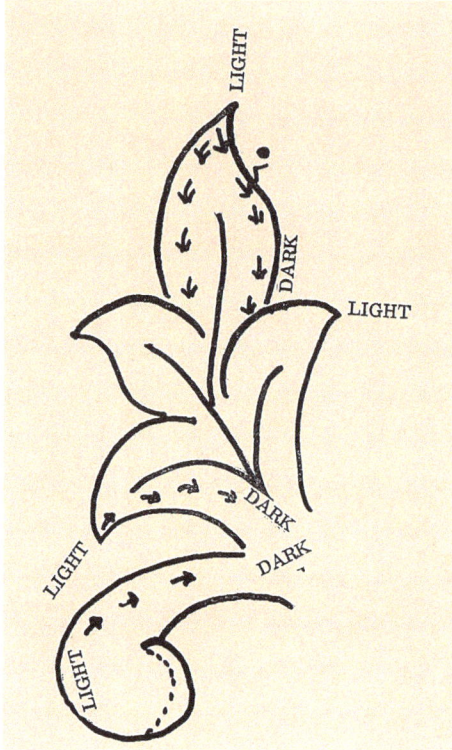

Fig. 4

Original 1964 Book Image

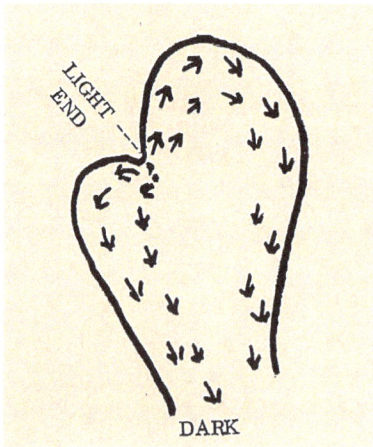

Fig. 5

Original 1964 Book Image

Suggestions For Other
Types Of Scrolls

Your rug may have a very large leafy scroll and you might like to dye over more than six colors. Why not use two values of some colors, one very light and the other a little darker to dye over? Use the darker shades in the fingers at the base of the scroll and gradually use lighter hues as you go to the top. Another suggestion would be to dye over related colors like white, beige, yellow, medium yellow and gold. For geometrics or a small scroll you may not need as great a variety of colors. Three or four pastels would be enough. I think dyeing over pastels enhances your colors. For leaves try dyeing over yellow and blue as well as white and beige and use them all in the same rug. In fact, even on the same branch, it adds interest to your flowers.

Two formulas can be used in the same scroll, especially if the No. 3 dye is the same or similar. This fits into a large flowing scroll rather than a smaller one. Another way would be to use, for example, gold No. 1, woodrose No. 2 and bronze green No. 3 for one set of swatches and woodrose No. 1, gold No. 2 and bronze green No. 3 for a second set. Just by interchanging your No. 1 and No. 2 dyes you would have twelve colors in your scroll rather than six, still using the same three dyes. There are so many possibilities, I know some of you will come up with many new ideas.

678-3

Laverne Brescia Photo

Planning Your Rug

When making a rug with a scroll, plan the scroll colors first. It determines the colors for the entire rug. There must be a close relationship between the scroll and the center of the rug. Therefore, some of the scroll swatches MUST be used for some of the flowers and leaves. Small amounts of other dyes can be used along with your scroll colors to give your flowers more character. For example, suppose you used gold rust and mahogany in the scroll. One flower could be mahogany or a combination of mahogany, rust and terra cotta which peps up the flowers etc.

Round Footstool - Pearl McGown Design #60

Laverne Brescia Photo

Rugs With Scrolls

"FOREVER YOUNG"
Original 1964 Book Image

Forever Young (McGown Design No. 747)

Formula and material:
No. 1, Gold- ¼ teaspoon
No. 2, Woodrose- ¼ teaspoon
No. 3, Bronze green- ¼ teaspoon minus ⅟₃₂
3x16 strips dyed over white, beige, yellow, pink, blue and green.
4 pieces of each color.

Tulips- made with yellow scroll swatch. Start with light end at top of petal and hook to base.

Tulip and Iris leaves- (strap leaves), made with blue swatch. Lightest end at tip and hook to base.

Roses- Woodrose- ½ teaspoon; Gold scant ⅔₂ teaspoon. Stock Solution. Make 8 shades and then overdye with 1 teaspoon of bronze green solution (made with ½ teaspoon bronze green in ½ cup of water).

Iris- (Top Petals), Gold- ¼ teaspoon; Bronze green ⅟₃₂ teaspoon. Stock Solution.

Dip dye over white and yellow material; 4 teaspoons stock solution to 6 pieces of material (4 x length of petal).

Iris- (Bottom Petals), use rose formula with ¹⁄₃₂ teaspoon mahogany dye added for sparkle.

Rose Leaves- Bronze green- ½ teaspoon; Gold ¹⁄₃₂ teaspoon.   Stock Solution.

Dip dyed over blue; 6 strips 3x12 dipped in 8 teaspoons of stock solution. Since the blue material was used for turnovers on the scroll, all the rose leaves were dyed over blue.

Background- was light beige overdyed with rose leaf formula, four teaspoons of stock solution to one pound of material. Color is set with salt.

You will notice that there is bronze green and gold in all the formulas. It seems to give the rug a certain muted glow which is pleasing.

The Scroll- is a fist scroll. Hence, you must have a dark shade to put inside under the fingers.

Shadow Inside Scroll- dye four pieces of blue 16x16 by placing No. 1 dye, ¼ teaspoon of gold in a pan of boiling water with ½ cup of vinegar. Boil until water is clear. Lift material and add No. 2 dye, woodrose ¼ teaspoon with ½ cup of vinegar. When water is clear again lift out material and add No. 3 dye, bronze green and last ½ cup of vinegar but increase the No. 3 dye to ½ teaspoon to make it darker than the base of the fingers.

This rug takes three complete 24 piece swatches plus one more swatch made with only the colors you use most of- my 4th swatch was 2 blue, 2 beige and 2 yellow. In other words you will have 8 pieces of blue, 8 of beige and 8 of yellow.

After your flowers are hooked take bits of the lighter scroll materials and tuck on edges of some of the petals. I put the green on edges of rose petals, gold and pink on leaf edges and some of the rose colors on the gold Iris petals. Your flowers come alive when these little jewels are tucked in here and there on petals and leaves.

"GAINSBOROUGH"
Original 1964 Book Image

Gainsborough (McGown Design No. 440). This rug is 60" round and has a very beautiful scroll.

Formula and materials:
No. 1, Gold- ¼ teaspoon
No. 2, Rust- ¼ teaspoon
No. 3, Mahogany- ¼ teaspoon minus ⅟₃₂
Dyed over white, yellow, pink, beige, blue and green.
Pastel strips 3x18. It will take six 24 piece swatches for rug.

The Scroll Knobs were made with the blue swatch, other colors placed in a pleasing harmony throughout scroll.

The Peacock Eyes. Put four pieces of beige, 16x18, on your coat hanger and dye as you did for scroll with the same dyes. Take the dyed pieces and fold in thirds and cut. Your pieces are now 6x16 giving you a light, medium and dark shade. Hook 2 or 3 rows of light color on outside edge of peacock eye. Then the medium shade and dark shade on inside. Fill in with background (see photo on page 28 and Fig. 6, page 29).

"Gainsborough"
Laverne Brescia Photo

Rose- Mahogany- ½ teaspoon; Rust- ¹⁄₁₆ teaspoon; Terra Cotta- ¹⁄₁₆ teaspoon. 8 shades over white.

Foxglove- darker shades of rose colors.

Small Tulips- yellow scroll material.

Large Tulips- painted dyeing, using gold at one end, mahogany at the other end, and center rust; overlap gold and mahogany with rust.

Chrysanthemum- Gold- ½ teaspoon; Rose Pink- ¹⁄₁₆ teaspoon; Aqua- ¹⁄₁₆ teaspoon. 8 shades over white. Spot some of the darker shades with rust to be used for shadow.

Ferns- scroll material, yellow, beige, pink and green.

Oak Leaves- blue scroll material.

Rose Leaves- Bronze green- 1 teaspoon; Dark green- ¹⁄₃₂ teaspoon. Dip dyed over blue.

Background- various dark browns overdyed with dark brown and mahogany. Formula- 4 parts dark brown, 1 part mahogany.

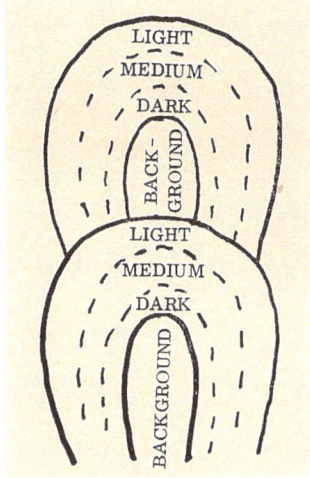

Fig. 6

Original 1964 Book Image

"Gainsborough"

Judith Brescia-Keenan Photo

GEOMETRICS

Some geometric designs lend themselves beautifully to this type of dyeing. Use just one pastel or more to dye over.

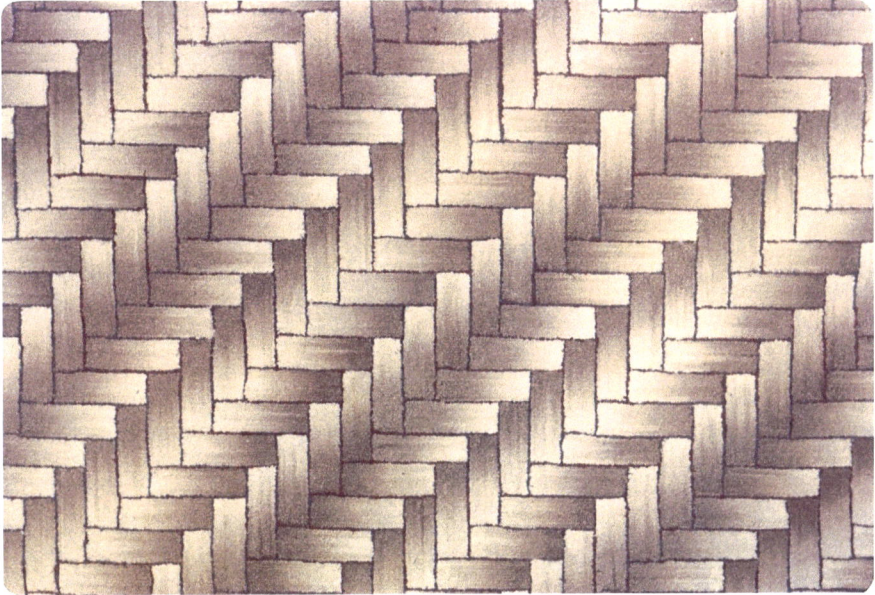

"POSTCARD"

Laverne Brescia Photo

Post Card (McGown Design No. 215). 34¾" x 54⅛"

Formula:
No. 1, Nugget gold- ¹⁄₁₆ teaspoon
No. 2, Salmon- ¹⁄₁₆ teaspoon
No. 3, Seal brown- ¹⁄₁₆ teaspoon
Over white 3x13. It takes 4½ swatches of 24 pieces each.

All chevrons are outlined in a plaid. One row of chevrons hooked from light to dark, the next row hooked from dark to light. It is very easy to do and doesn't get monotonous. This is an old design but shading it this way gives it a modern look.

"CROSS & ROSES"

Laverne Brescia Photo

Cross & Roses (McGown Design No. SD-2). Diagonal rows of simple crosses with a flat conventional flower between.

Formula:

No. 1, Woodrose- ¼ teaspoon

No. 2, Khaki drab- ⁴⁄₃₂ teaspoon

No. 3, Garnet- ¼ teaspoon minus ¹⁄₃₂.

Dyed over 6 white, 6 yellow, 6 pink, and 6 beige. Strips 3x18.

All crosses were outlined with aqua and rose texture. Two arms of cross were made in white and the other two in pink. The neighboring cross was made of yellow and beige. Alternate colors throughout rug (see Fig. 7, page 33).

Conventional flowers- Formula: Turquoise green- ½ teaspoon; Aqualon blue- ¹⁄₁₆ teaspoon; Garnet- ¹⁄₁₆ teaspoon. Dyed over white, 8 shades. Little squares outlined in plaid, filled in with medium flower shades.

Background was black overdyed with garnet. A simple way to make this rug and a little different. It is a good beginner's pattern.

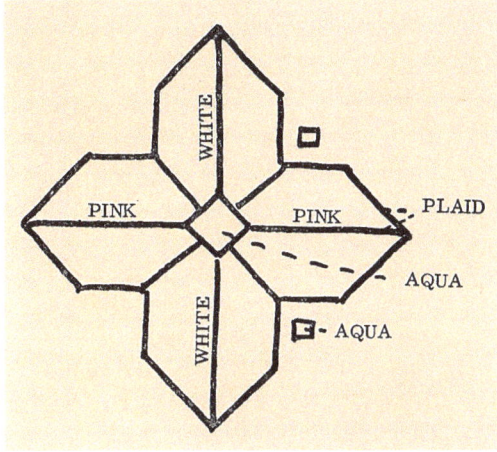

Fig. 7

Original 1964 Book Image

PILLOW TOP

McGown Design No. 4
Original 1964 Book Image

Formula:

No. 1, Woodrose - ¼ teaspoon

No. 2, Khaki drab - ⁴⁄₃₂ teaspoon

No. 3, Garnet - ¼ teaspoon minus ⅓₂.

Dyed over 6 of each white, yellow, beige and pink

Veins - very dull tannish brown.

Background - black.

Laverne Brescia Photo

FOOTSTOOL

McGown Design No. 43

Original 1964 Book Image

Formula:

No. 1, Gold - ¼ teaspoon

No. 2, Apricot - ¼ teaspoon

No. 3, Green - ¼ teaspoon minus ⅟₃₂

Dyed over white, yellow, beige, pink, blue, and green.

Vein - tan material spotted with apricot and green.

Background - very dark dull green, as is material.

* This is the type of scroll that is easier to make if you trace with a marker one branch at a time and then hook.

Laverne Brescia Photo

Helpful Hints

If you have a scroll that consists of many sprays or branches, one coming out from the other, try tracing one branch with the magic marker and hook it- this blots out all the rest. Then trace another branch and hook. It helps simplify the design and you can see what you are doing. Start with the branch on top and work the back branches last.

If you feel timid about hooking your scroll, trace a small section on burlap and practice. It is easier and better to rip on your sampler and does not harm the rug burlap. An easy way to trace a pattern is as follows: Trace the design on tracing paper. Next place a piece of cheap, rather stiff, nylon net curtain material over your traced design. Scotch tape the net curtain material securely so it won't slip. Trace on the curtain with the magic marker the design you can see through the curtain material from the original tracing. Now place the curtain material with the transcribed design over your burlap. Pin in place and make certain it is straight. Go over your design again with the magic marker and you have a nice clear dark tracing on your burlap.

Flowers can also be made with this type of dyeing. Make your strips four times the length of petal. Start at top with the lightest shade and hook in contour to base of petals. Your shading comes in automatically. Where one petal goes under another you may have to cut or pull up loops to get to darker shades. It is an easy way to make certain flowers with better results. Roses, tulips and iris are a few that are beautifully made this way. Don't forget to tuck your bits of color at the edges of some of your petals. I usually add these after the flower is finished. Place your rug on the back of a chair, then stand back and you can usually see where your little sparkles or jewels of color should go. Experiment - you learn more that way and have fun. Try it, your flowers really come alive. Leaves - use your scroll materials for leaves, especially the long strap leaves such as tulip, iris, etc. The long strips fit better in these without too much snipping. Large leaves or Autumn leaves can be made with this method of dyeing.

I hope this little book will help you with your scrolls. They are comparatively easy to make and my students are having fun hooking them. Scrolls are as easy as "painting with numbers".

Visit www.ScrollsAreEasy.com for examples of rugs in full color, and/or to purchase more copies of this publication.

FORMULAS

1

Coral	¼ teaspoon
Yellow	¼ teaspoon
Green	¼ teaspoon (minus ⅓₂ teaspoon)

2

Peacock	¼ teaspoon
Strawberry	¼ teaspoon
Bright Green	¼ teaspoon (minus ⅓₂ teaspoon)

3

Chartreuse	¼ teaspoon
Coral	¼ teaspoon
Medium Brown	¼ teaspoon (minus ⅓₂ teaspoon)

4

Gold	¼ teaspoon
Rust	¼ teaspoon
Mahogany	¼ teaspoon (minus ⅓₂ teaspoon)

5

Nugget Gold	¼ teaspoon
Salmon	¼ teaspoon
Seal Brown	¼ teaspoon

6

Nugget Gold	¼ teaspoon
Salmon	¼ teaspoon
Green	¼ teaspoon (minus ⅟₃₂ teaspoon)

7

Gold	¼ teaspoon
Apricot	¼ teaspoon
Bronze Green	¼ teaspoon

8

Woodrose	¼ teaspoon
Khaki Drab	⁴⁄₃₂ teaspoon
Garnet	¼ teaspoon (minus ⅟₃₂ teaspoon)

9

Gold	¼ teaspoon
Bronze	¼ teaspoon
Dark Green	¼ teaspoon (minus ⅟₃₂ teaspoon)

10

Apricot	¼ teaspoon
Rust	¼ teaspoon
Brown	¼ teaspoon

11

Apricot	¼ teaspoon
Woodrose	¼ teaspoon
Brown Rust	¼ teaspoon

12

Gold	¼ teaspoon
Navy	$3/32$ teaspoon
Mahogany	¼ teaspoon (minus $1/32$ teaspoon)

13

Gold	¼ teaspoon
Salmon	¼ teaspoon
Mahogany	¼ teaspoon (minus $1/32$ teaspoon)

14

Old Gold	¼ teaspoon
Old Rose	¼ teaspoon
Olive	¼ teaspoon (minus $1/32$ teaspoon)

15

Taupe	¼ teaspoon
Reseda	¼ teaspoon
Mahogany	⅛ teaspoon

16

Nile Green	¼ teaspoon
Sky Blue	¼ teaspoon
Cardinal	⅛ teaspoon

17

Apricot	¼ teaspoon
Woodrose	¼ teaspoon
Mahogany	¼ teaspoon (minus $\frac{1}{32}$ teaspoon)

In Loving Memory of Laverne E. Brescia

1905 - 2003

Photographer Unknown

www.ingramcontent.com/pod-product-compliance
Lightning Source LLC
LaVergne TN
LVHW010026070426
835509LV00001B/23